AF442769

The
Hidden
Chronicle.

Copyright © <2024> <Samprita Swaminathan>

All Rights Reserved.

This book has been self-published with all reasonable efforts taken to make the material error-free by the author. No part of this book shall be used, reproduced in any manner whatsoever without written permission from the author, except in the case of brief quotations embodied in critical articles and reviews.

The Author of this book is solely responsible and liable for its content including but not limited to the views, representations, descriptions, statements, information, opinions and references ["Content"]. The Content of this book shall not constitute or be construed or deemed to reflect the opinion or expression of the Publisher or Editor. Neither the Publisher nor Editor endorse or approve the Content of this book or guarantee the reliability, accuracy or completeness of the Content published herein and do not make any representations or warranties of any kind, express or implied, including but not limited to the implied warranties of merchantability, fitness for a particular purpose. The Publisher and Editor shall not be liable whatsoever for any errors, omissions, whether such errors or omissions result from negligence, accident, or any other cause or claims for loss or damages of any kind, including without limitation, indirect or consequential loss or damage arising out of use, inability to use, or about the reliability, accuracy or sufficiency of the information contained in this book.

Dedicated to every young adult out there

who doesn't know what they are feeling

Author's note,

This book is a collation of years' worth of poems, it depicts a journey through an adolescent's mind. It's a timeline of being in vain, undergoing change and ultimately healing from emotional wounds.

It goes through issues that we as teenagers face and coping mechanisms that we use, some of the content may be triggering for some audience so I implore that you go through the trigger warning section before proceeding with the book

<u>Trigger Warnings</u>

- Body dysmorphia

- Self-hatred

- Mental illness

- Self-harm

- Mild mentions of eating disorders

- Indirect mentions of suicidal ideations

Contents

The onset

- Number one
- Person
- Just teens
- My turn
- Friend
- Unwanted
- Twisted trust

Amidst the chaos

- Weather
- Lone
- Poison
- Alienate
- Tiny things
- Perceive
- The things I wonder
- A couple of minutes
- Windows
- Feelings
- Who I am

- Antarctic winter

- Brute

- Hiding

- Downpour

The Realization

- Complaining

- A broken mirror

- Little girl

- Surreal

- Tethered

- Remember

- Advantage

- Humans

- My wish

- Learning

- Growing up

- Goodbye

The onset:

The onset takes us through the beginning of the downfall. How the transition of going from a child to a teen feels. As we develop more feelings and emotions and learn that the world isn't black and white but shades of grey.

1

Number One

The onset

Always be number **one.**

Stay up till **two** and study.

After only **three** hours of sleep,

And **four** nightmares later,

Time to wake up at **five,**

Just to do **six** hours of school.

Be there by **seven.**

Eight assignments to finish,

Nine different classes to attend every day,

And **Ten** extra curriculars to keep up with.

If that's what it takes to be number **one,**

Then that's what I will do.

2

Person

The onset

Everyone needs a person they trust,

Even more so than themself.

Someone who cares in times of unjust,

When u lay in your inner delf.

Someone who saves you as you combust.

Holds you as you fall off the shelf.

I'm always that person,

But when will I find my person.

3

Just Teens

The onset

We may just be teens,

but the expectations are obscene.

Who am I, if not lean,

with the structure of a small figurine.

Appear so sheen,

so much so that every pore is clean.

Our struggles unseen,

but when notice blamed on our screens.

We live in chaos that can't be seen,

but we too need our moments of serene.

4

My turn

The onset

Will it ever be my turn?

Always the poet,

but never the poem.

Always the artist,

but never the art.

Always just heard off,

but never truly seen.

All I wish for,

is to be taken in,

to be the Muse for once.

Be the Story,

In some author's novel.

Oh, but I wonder,

will it ever be my turn?

5

That Friend

The onset

I need that friend.

That friend who is ready,

to sit through my tantrums.

That friend who is ready,

to listen to my little burbles.

That friend who is ready,

to walk with me through all I fear.

That friend who is ready,

to be with me for the remaining moments of my life.

I will find that friend,

regardless of how long it takes.

6

Unwanted

The onset

She was the puddle,

because of the convulsive rain.

She was the wind,

because of the vicious storm.

She was the sound,

because of the brooding thunder.

However, she was never,

the succeeding rainbow,

that people wanted.

7

Twisted Trust

The onset

How does one know whom to trust,

when words mean as little as dust.

Vulnerability, something I fear.

because what if they talk right behind my back.

Accepting a person in your life,

something I will never begin,

because I know they will leave me all alone again.

My brain twisted,

Just like the rest of me,

twists every tale that ever transpires,

and I still believe despite knowing that,

it is by far the biggest liar...

Amidst the chaos:

This delves into the darkest of times.

It walks us through the chaos, that is caused by our own mind

and showcase some painfully raw emotions.

8

Weather

Amidst the chaos

The weather inside of me,

why is it so different,

than the one outside me.

The one outside being,

the bold rays of the sun,

blessing the surface of the earth.

The cool breezy wind,

brushing past me at every striking second.

But what so ever,

The weather within me is a whirlwind.

My tiny heart consumed by,

the dark and stormy clouds that surround it.

The oceans rising until,

my eyes can no longer contain them.

After all this,

I am left with that empty silence,

that enclasp after the storm has passed.

9

Lone

Amidst the chaos

There is a fine line between,

being alone and feeling lonely.

Some people choose to be alone,

they embraced it and have grown.

However, I did not choose this life for myself.

Always a part of a group,

and yet left out of the loop.

Taken for granted,

am I really gullible,

or simply just invisible.

Someone new comes along,

am I that easy to replace,

our friendship was so easily defaced.

It is points like this where the line blurs,

Because things can never go back to the way they were.

10

Poison

Amidst the chaos

We were always told to stay away from poison,

But what if I am my own poison.

My mind my own prison.

My thoughts all in negative foison.

Then tell me,

How the hell do I stay away from poison.

11

Alienate

Amidst the chaos

Oh well here we go again,

Let the seclusion begin.

 As I let everything, I've worked for perish,

And all my lies in high embellish.

I stand there helpless,

In my pool of worthless,

As I alienate the ones that care enough.

I don't wish for you to see me as I mess up.

I don't wish for you to see me when I'm low.

I don't wish for you to see me as a disappointment.

And so, I push you away.

And pray to God you will stay...

12

Tiny Things

Amidst the chaos

It's the tiny things,

that makes a person who they are,

that makes a person feel a certain way.

A tiny gesture by a loved one,

enough to create a feeling of joy,

Joy strong enough to mask any other emotion.

A tiny trigger caused by anything,

just as easily cause a hurricane.

One that makes your heart,

shatter into a million pieces.

Everything you worked for,

crash and burn to the floor.

In that moment,

everything seems so overwhelming.

This is the feeling that consumes u from within,

just like a hurricane...

13

Perceive

Amidst the chaos

I can't stand to look in the mirror,

in fear of what I may see.

Is what I perceive an illusion,

made up by pure delusion.

Is what I perceive how I resemble,

if so every part of my body,

I wish to disassemble.

I go back to bed,

wondering if it is all in my head.

I will never know,

because all I'll ever perceive,

is this hideous version of my own.

14

The Things I Wonder

Amidst the chaos

I wonder if anyone knows...

Feeling of entering a room,

and feeling inferior to every person there.

The feeling of your own thoughts.

screaming you're your own useless.

The feeling of that unfiltered pure rage,

coursing through your veins.

The feeling of punching something,

till but the pain renders your arm immobile.

But most of all,

I wonder if my own brain knows,

the damage it is imposing on me and itself.

15

A couple of minutes

Amidst the chaos

For a minute that day,

 I shattered so hard.

I was petrified someone heard it.

Only for a minute though,

because the next,

 I had to pick up the pieces,

and hide them in my heart,

So, no one sees it.

16

Window

Amidst the chaos

Am I truly experiencing each moment,

or am I watching life pass by through a window.

I watch the time go around over and over again,

I watch the seasons changes,

I watch the date change,

I watch myself change,

but that's just it,

I can only watch.

Like I have zero control over my presence in this world.

One day I locked my emotions behind a façade,

and I can't seem to find the key anymore.

Maybe I will feel alive for once,

after I crack open and jump out that window.

17

Feelings

Amidst the chaos

I feel nothing,

I feel something,

I feel everything,

whatever I feel,

I feel all too much.

My biggest fortitude,

and my biggest downfall.

A fragment of happiness,

enough to ignite an inferno of felicity.

A mere misdemeanour,

enough to spark a blazing conflagration.

I feel so much,

only to be burned by both...

18

Who I am

Amidst the chaos

I am haunted,

by thoughts from the past,

and feelings that shouldn't last.

I am wounded,

by words I never said,

and things I never did.

I am afraid,

of just being tossed,

or even simply feeling lost.

I am aware,

of my dreadful fate,

that merely refuses to fade.

But none of this reflects who I am.

The real me is trapped

beneath several layers,

of betrayed trust and pure rage,

and I will be damned if I ever show it.

19

Antarctic Winters

Amidst the chaos

Physically I am present here,

a tropical land, filled with bright days and brighter colours.

However deep down, I live in Antarctica.

When people say every night will have a brighter day,

I don't think they realize Antarctica doesn't see a brighter day that often.

It survives in darkness for six months that feel like forever,

forever of a cold, stale and empty void.

No Sense of warmth to the eye's reach.

During these winters the Isolation one feels is painful,

when the ice around the island freezes

letting no one in or out of the island.

that's exactly how I feel,

I am Stuck.

Stuck with people from 3 years ago, who brought me here

unable to let them out. unable to let people in.

Cuz that's Just how it is.

20

Brute

Amidst the chaos

I'm in danger more,

because of the monsters in my head,

over even the ones under my bed.

I scare myself more,

with the voices in my head,

then the ones of the dead.

I hurt myself more,

because of the things I tell myself in my head,

then over anything you have ever said.

So, tell me am I the victim,

or am I the brute.

21

Hiding

Amidst the chaos

I've spent years hiding,

yet I find myself uncertain,

from what it is that I am hiding from.

My own mind,

the whole truth,

or the people in my life.

What so ever the reason might be,

one day I do hope,

I pull back the curtains,

and face whatever it is that I'm hiding from.

Or I am too debilitated for even that.

22

Downpour

Amidst the chaos

The brooding clouds,

the thunder aloud,

downpour like never seen before,

luring me into the great outdoors.

The seething rain engulfing me,

screaming to the void "just let me be".

Just like the fields my mind inundate,

thoughts all escaping through the flood gates.

At last peace and quiet all I hear,

just like my mind only now clear.

The realization

This is what is left of you after the chaos.

The realization and the remains.

Healing and learning to love those shades of grey.

23

Complaining

The realization

The moon all alone,

I do not hear it complaining.

The night never asleep,

I do not hear it complaining.

The earth always spinning,

I don't hear it complaining.

But I hear myself complaining.

About being lonely,

about not being able to sleep,

about my head always spinning.

But it never occurs to me,

that I brought this upon myself.

24

Brute

The realization

Falling apart, it is normal.

Some manage to pick up the pieces and some don't.

But what they don't realize,

is that they are picking up pieces of a broken mirror.

The more they put together the more they see,

beyond the cracks,

beyond the mess,

beyond it all.

They start seeing who they really are.

For all of their pretty,

and all of their flaws.

At that instant,

there is no hiding and escaping,

from that mirror or the truth,

that you are being faced with.

That's when you realize how messed up

everything really is and how there is no going back.

25

Little Girl

The realization

Everyone says "I miss my old self".

Expect I'm not sure that version of me,

would survive it all over again unscathed.

She was the little girl,

that wouldn't leave her parents side out of fear.

She was the little girl,

whose frivolousness was dismissed by her own friends.

she was the little girl,

that saw her perfect A's slide into D's .

she was the little girl,

that was sidestepped at every chance of hers.

She was the little girl,

that I never wish returns.

26

Surreal

The realization

It all so surreal,

as I look for the key.

I yearn to heal,

from wounds that you can't see.

I yearn to feel,

emotions that will set me free.

I yearn to deal,

with my phantom mental debris.

I yearn to zeal,

to happiness which I guarantee.

It all is so surreal,

something I could never foresee.

27

Tethered

The realization

Why am I so tethered to my past,

a past that I loathe.

Years of being an outcast,

forgotten in the undergrowth.

The days passing by anything but fast,

tiring physically and mentally both.

I escaped all the horror at last.

An agonizing emotional growth.

28

Remember

The realization

I don't remember,

when "Can I have another cookie"

became "I can't have even one cookie".

I don't remember,

when "This dress should fit me"

became "I should fit into this dress".

I don't remember,

when Buying things by looking at the colours,

became buying things by looking at the calories.

But I do remember,

I was so much happier,

before I thought this would all make me prettier.

29

Advantage

The realization

I have always noticed the little things,

that never played out to my advantage.

Upon years of dealing with that damage,

I have finally learned how to manage.

I have always noticed the little things.

And only now let myself see,

the advantages that it brings.

30

My wish

The realization

I'm treating people in a way,

I wish I was treated once.

I'm helping people in a way,

I wish I was helped once.

I'm telling people things,

I wish I had heard once.

I'm always there even if no one was there,

for me at my absolute worst.

I'm healing people in any way I can,

even though I could never heal myself.

I do all of this even if it is draining me

because no one should go through this,

the way I did.

Because in the end we are all just wounded Souls.

Some are just better at hiding it that the others.

31

Humans

The realization

Humans, I suppose,

are a diluted reflection of the earth.

From the tears representing the rain,

to the cellulite depicting the cracks of the earth.

From our Veins mirroring roots,

to our hair fallen like pretty vines.

The earth is truly beautiful,

so why believe we are otherwise?

32

Learning

The realization

I never thought I will be 16 and learning.

Learning to eat,

learning to breathe,

learning to live.

I never thought I will be 16,

and learning that I wouldn't have it any other way.

33

Growing up

The realization

I take a step back

and at last,

I feel content with my life.

I feel at peace with who I am.

I know that I am not perfect,

but I also understand that I need not be.

I know what matters,

and how much I let it affect me.

I know whom to trust,

and how to let go and be free.

I look back to see,

I see a little girl,

and only then that do I realize,

That this is called growing up.

34

Goodbye

The realization

Goodbye I say.

To the moody days,

and the gloomy haze.

To the bitter thoughts,

and the twisted knots.

To rotten memories,

and dire reveries.

Goodbye I scream,

to the low spirits,

that I now command,

to stay away.

About the author...

Samprita Swaminathan is a dynamic 16-year-old high schooler whose passion for creativity knows no bounds. As a first-time author, Samprita strives to bring a difference to the world through her words. Beyond her literary pursuits, she is deeply involved in social work, which only further demonstrates her commitment to making a positive impact in her community.

Music is one of the main parts of her life, she is a skilled singer and songwriter with almost a decade in Carnatic, Hindustani, and Western music, this displays her commitment and versatility. Dance is another avenue of expression for Samprita. From Bharatanatyam to hip-hop, she's been honing her skills for seven years, showcasing her talent through performances. And let's not forget theatre. Having done both acting and play writing, Samprita has spent five years practicing this craft and was recently certified in the same.

Samprita is artistically well versed and wishes to make her mark in the worlds of literature, music, dance, theatre and design.

Epilogue

I want to express my deepest gratitude to everyone who has joined me in this adventure. Pouring my heart into this book has been an incredibly fulfilling experience. I hope that through these poems, you found moments that resonated with you, that made you feel seen, and perhaps, offered some comfort and understanding.

To my readers, thank you for taking the time to explore my words and for allowing me to share my world with you. Your support means everything to me.

To my parents, thank you for your unwavering belief in me and for always encouraging me to pursue my passions. Your motivation has been my driving force.

And to my brother, thank you for being my relentless support, for always standing by me, and for cheering me on through every challenge and triumph.

This book is not just a collection of poems, it is a piece of my heart. Thank you for being a part of it.

Loads of love,

Samprita Swaminathan.

www.ingramcontent.com/pod-product-compliance
Lightning Source LLC
Chambersburg PA
CBHW031244130726
47988CB00008B/3231